D0108887

his princess
girl talk with God

LOVE LETTERS AND DEVOTIONS
FOR YOUNG WOMEN

sheri rose shepherd

Revell

a division of Baker Publishing Group
Grand Rapids, Michigan

Published by Revell
a division of Baker Publishing Group
P.O. Box 6287, Grand Rapids, MI 49516-6287
www.revellbooks.com

Printed in the United States of America

Library of Congress Cataloging-in-Publication Data
Shepherd, Sheri Rose, 1961–
    His princess girl talk with God : love letters and devotions for young
women / Sheri Rose Shepherd.
        p.   cm.
    Includes bibliographical references.
    ISBN 978-0-8007-1952-4 (cloth)
    1. Teenage girls—Religious life. 2. Christian teenagers—Religious
life. I. Title.
BV4551.3.S548 2010
242'.633—dc22   2010003581

10   11   12   13   14   15   16   8   7   6   5   4   3   2

Contents

I want to dedicate this book to
my daughter Emilie Joy Shepherd and
my daughter-in-law Amanda Shepherd.

You both are the best examples I know
of young women who have
a true heart for God.

Introduction

His Princesses Are Not Perfect

I know how hard it is for us to think of ourselves as royalty. Each of us knows our weaknesses and imperfections all too well! So let me take the pressure off you: No man or woman in the Bible or in Christian history, no believer who did something great to further God's kingdom, lived a perfect life. And despite their failures and insecurities, God loved them and chose them to conquer difficulties and achieve something great in their life.

I have discovered God is not looking for perfect princesses and He loves us girls no matter what we wear, what we say, what we do, or how we feel. You don't have to earn His love and approval. He just wants to love you.

By the grace of God, I wrote this book for you because so many of you asked for it. In the following pages, we'll get into some "girl talk with God" in forty devotionals. Each one starts with a story from my life that I hope will be helpful to you in your walk with God. Following that is what I call a Love Letter from God—it's what God might say to you if He were writing you a letter. This is something that the Lord has always pressed upon my heart for women, and now He's pressed it upon my heart for you, to show you how much He loves you. And each devotional includes a special Scripture.

My prayer for you as we dive into these scriptural love letters and girl talk devotions is that you will grab hold of how much you are treasured by your "Daddy in heaven." If you get this truth, you will want to do whatever your Father asks of you—not because of some kind of religious guilt but because you have a God who has amazing plans for your life.

Sheri Rose Shepherd

> God can do anything, you know—far more
> than you could ever imagine or guess or
> request in your wildest dreams!
>
> Ephesians 3:20 Message

1

The Crowning Moment

The bright lights were shining in my eyes. My heart raced as I stood in front of an audience, waiting to see who would win the crown at this national beauty pageant. Among those two thousand audience members were my family and friends who knew how much I had to overcome in my life to be standing on that stage at this moment. The countdown began with the fourth runner-up and continued until the moment of affirmation I'd dreamed of all my life arrived—the master of ceremonies called my name as the national winner on live TV. I cried as that crown was placed on my head and the crystal-beaded banner was hung over my shoulder. Cameras flashed, people applauded, and women gathered around me to celebrate my victory. It seemed like a dream.

When the cameras stopped flashing and the audience emptied out of the auditorium, I walked back to my hotel room. I took off the crown and laid it on the table by the window. I turned off the lights and saw that the crystal crown sparkled with the reflection of the full moon's light. As I stared at the beautiful crown that I had so longed for, I began to remember a different time, a different hotel room. It had happened ten years earlier. I had felt hopeless and desperate for someone or something to fill my empty soul. At that time in my life, I had all the things that should have meant happiness and fulfillment. I had overcome a drug problem, I had lost sixty pounds, and I owned my own modeling production company. I had lots of money, shopping sprees, beauty titles, boyfriends, and cool clothes. I drove a nice car and had a calendar full of places to go and people to see.

On the outside I looked like I had it all together, but on the inside I was falling apart. I battled depression and bulimia. I felt empty and alone even when I was in a crowd of people. I could not find anything or anyone to fill that deep lonely place in my heart. I began to feel as if I had nothing to live for. So I checked into that hotel room with plans to end my life with an overdose of sleeping pills. I fell to the floor and I cried out to God as my last hope. He heard my cry and rescued me before I took my life. I actually felt God's holy presence with me in the room, and for the first time in my life, I did not feel alone. Instead I felt loved and at peace.

That night was my true crowning moment, because God gave me the greatest crown of all—not a crown given by a panel of judges, but the crown of everlasting life given by my Daddy in heaven. I finally had the love and attention I was searching for.

As exciting as winning a national crown was, that amazing event pales in comparison to the night the King welcomed me into His family as His much-loved daughter.

If God wrote a love letter to you . . .

My beautiful girl—

Although I am God, I am also your Daddy in heaven. You are My precious daughter and my amazing creation. I had you on My mind before you were born. I know everything about you, and I love My girl. I am here for you, to meet your every need and to help you find your dream. You are My chosen child, and I have great plans for you now and in the future. One day we will see each other face-to-face—Father and daughter—and you will experience the wonderful place I have prepared for you in heaven. But for now I want you to know that you are loved and I am with you always. Although I am God, My arms are not too big to hold you, My beloved daughter.

Love,
Your Daddy in heaven

And I will be your Father,
   and you will be my sons and daughters,
   says the Lord Almighty.

2 Corinthians 6:18

2

Your True Identity

When I reflect back on my teen years, I often think of the time I wasted allowing my friends to define my worth. Two memories are especially painful. One is our homecoming king calling me "Sheri the Whale" at a prom; the other is my English teacher telling me I was born to lose in life.

I was so broken by their words that I did whatever I could to prove my worth. In one year I went from being a drug-using, overweight, insecure junior in high school to a powerful, popular senior who had boyfriends, a local beauty title, and what seemed like a much better place in life. It looked like I had it all. But I was still empty and insecure. It didn't matter how much I projected a perfect life or look on the outside, because deep down inside I battled with hidden depression and an eating disorder. And I was addicted to people's approval of me.

Popularity, attention, beauty, and cool clothes could hide my pain but could not heal my broken heart or rebuild my family after my parents' divorce. It was not until I was more desperate for God's love than my friends' approval and praise that I finally found my true identity. How we feel about ourselves does not change our true identity in Christ.

Today I have traded lies for truth, and I am free to be who I was created to be. My English teacher did not teach what I call God's Grammar Lesson: "Don't put a period where He has a comma, because He has a plan for every life He creates."

I was not born to lose, and neither were you.

If God wrote a love letter to you . . .

My beautiful girl—

I know that your true identity is under great attack every day. Voices all around you tell you to become like the world and surrender who you really are. Don't let anyone define you but Me, your Daddy in heaven. You are a daughter of the King, and you don't have to become someone you don't want to be. You will never find your true identity looking at idols of this world. Don't allow these lies to control your confidence anymore. I created you in My image. My daughter does not have to bow down to man-made images in magazines. How you feel about yourself does not change the truth that you are My treasured daughter. You are called to be a light in the dark and to help your friends find their worth in Me.

Love,
Your Daddy in heaven

"For I know the plans I have for you," declares the LORD, "plans to prosper you and not to harm you, plans to give you a hope and a future."

Jeremiah 29:11 NIV

3

Are You in Barbie Bondage?

I was born to parents who graduated from Hollywood High School in Southern California. My dad was a popular disc jockey who hosted beauty pageants. My mom was an actress, singer, and a Miss California. If anyone was ever destined to fall into Barbie Bondage, it was I.

Please don't misunderstand me: I have nothing against Mattel's Barbie doll. As a matter of fact, I'm kind of envious of her. She's a little miss hardbody without weight lifting; she wakes up with perfect makeup and no bed-head; she never says the wrong thing because she can't talk. So how did she ever get so popular?

Millions of young girls just like you—and me—learned their standard of beauty from this perky piece of plastic. I'm not saying we should banish Barbie. It's not her fault. She's only a symbol of what we see around us. And although Barbie doesn't talk, she has a message for all of us. It's the same message we see on television and in movies, music videos, and magazines. Though it comes to each of us in a whisper, the message rings loud and clear: "You are not pretty enough, and you need to perfect your body and your image."

When you hear something often enough—no matter if it's right or not—you begin to believe it. And when you feel something deeply and strongly, it will affect the way you think and act. We girls love to feel beautiful, and that's okay. But our minds are bombarded with so many mixed messages, it's hard to figure out who we're supposed to be or what true beauty is supposed to look like.

It's time to clear up the confusion and learn to be happy with who God created us to be.

If God wrote a love letter to you . . .

My beautiful girl—

I know you don't see yourself the way I do. You compare yourself to beauty idols that will soon be forgotten. If you could see yourself through My eyes, you would see that your beauty is a breath of heaven! When I look at you, I see a treasure ready to be discovered, a princess ready to shine. I have given you the kind of beauty that is everlasting, eternal. I lined your lips to speak words of life, and I have given you beautiful hands to reach out to your hurting friends. The beauty I had in mind when I created you is a reflection of Me. The beauty you possess will leave eternal marks on the hearts of all who were loved by you.

Love,
Your Daddy in heaven

Our daughters will be like pillars
carved to adorn a palace.

Psalm 144:12 NIV

4

How You Feel about Yourself

Here's the truth: Every one of God's girls has something inside her that cries out, "I want to make a difference with my life." You can be that girl who changes the world around you! The only thing that is holding you hostage from your heart's desire to become a super role model . . . is you!

We are Daughters of the King whether we believe it or not. Sadly some of us have traded our true identity in Christ for a tarnished version of ourselves fashioned by the approval of our friends. A low-cut dress or a navel ring or tattoo may get attention, but they can't buy love. Plastic surgery may change our appearance, but it can't change a heart. Expensive makeup may cover up our blemishes, but it won't hide our insecurities.

Don't misunderstand me. I think it's great to look your best—know what colors to wear, find your best haircut, eat healthy, and exercise. I'm all for making every effort to become the best version of you. But my prayer for you is that you are able to look in the mirror—not just at your face or your body, but at your heart. I pray you will be truly thankful for who you are.

That will free you to accomplish great things to further God's kingdom.

If God wrote a love letter to you . . .

My beautiful girl—

You are royalty even when you don't feel like a princess. How you feel about yourself will never change the truth of who you are. I have chosen you, and I am giving you a choice to choose Me over the world. If you are willing to choose Me, I am here. I believe in you and will wait for you until you are ready to step into your appointed position. I am well aware that you don't know where to start or how to become what I've called you to be. Start by recognizing who I am: the King of kings and Lord of lords and your Daddy in heaven. If you will make time to be still and pray and to read My Word each day, I will paint you a picture of the amazing life I have to offer you.

Love,
Your Daddy in heaven

You didn't choose me. I chose you. I appointed you to go and produce lasting fruit, so that the Father will give you whatever you ask for, using my name.

John 15:16

5

What You See Is What You'll Get

I heard the story of two girls who moved to a new city from two different towns. When they arrived at their new school, they were both curious about what the other kids were like in that school. The first girl asked the teacher about the other students, and the teacher asked her, "What kind of kids went to your old school?" The first girl said, "They were all rude, jealous, and mean." The teacher then told her that she would probably find the kids at this new school to be like the kids at her old school.

Later, the second girl approached the teacher and asked the same question: "What are the kids like here at this school?" The teacher replied, "What were the kids like at your old school?" The girl said, "They were really nice, fun, and friendly." The teacher said, "Well, I'm sure that's what kind of kids you'll see here."

Do you get the message? Beautiful eyes look for the best. Believe the best, and you'll find the best. When I walked around looking for what I could get from my friends, I always saw others as a disappointment. But when I began to see what I could give to my friends and family, I saw them as a gift.

Pray and ask God to give you His point of view and expect to see some great people in the world around you.

If God wrote a love letter to you . . .

My beautiful girl—

I know how hard it is for you to keep a good attitude and a tender heart in a harsh world. But I need you to be the light in the darkness, the one who will not give in to negativity. As your loving Father, I ask you to keep your eyes on Me so I can give you My view of the world around you. When you feel angry or hurt or disappointed, come to Me. Don't allow yourself to let emotions prevent you from seeing the blessings all around you. Ask Me to give you new sight to see the world through My eyes. And you will impact your friends and family.

Love,
Your Daddy in heaven

Above all else, guard your heart,
for everything you do flows from it.

Proverbs 4:23 TNIV

6

Never Enough

I won my first beauty title my senior year, and I could not wait to go to school the next day. I wanted to see that homecoming king who had humiliated me at my prom by calling me "Sheri the Whale." Mr. Popular would have to jump in the ocean of regret for what he said to me. I took several hours to get pretty for school that morning. I spent one hour on my makeup and another hour changing in and out of at least ten different outfits.

You would think that losing a lot of weight, winning a beauty title, and buying new clothes would make me feel self-confident. But it didn't. I began to live for words of praise about my new look. It felt great when I was being envied and adored, but I could never seem to get enough (kind of like chocolate). I became obsessed with tanning booths, working out twice a day, shopping daily for new outfits with Dad's credit card. At the peak of my quest for perfection, I won the "Best in Swimsuit Award" at Miss USA. This should have been enough to make me feel beautiful, but it didn't. I had it all and yet I was more insecure than when I was overweight in T-shirts and flip-flops with no makeup.

I joined the eight million girls in America who battle with an eating disorder. Six months into this self-destructive lifestyle, my eyes were always puffy and my head always hurt from throwing up—even my kidneys hurt. I cried myself to sleep every night, and then I put on a happy face for my family and friends. I was so ashamed of who I really was and how I felt. I could not bear the thought of telling anyone the truth—that I was out of control and losing it.

I can confidently tell you that external beauty, no matter how ravishing it may be, must have internal beauty and a godly purpose.

I pray that your inner beauty shines.

If God wrote a love letter to you . . .

My beautiful girl—

I know you want to be accepted by others, but I did not create you to fit in. I gave you the power to stand out by the way you live and love. You don't have to bow down to peer pressure to become popular. You are set apart, and I have given you all you need to feel loved and accepted. I don't want My daughter to waste another day, desperate for approval of others, or you will lose sight of your true identity. I want you to be one who feels secure in who you are. And I want you to help others find their acceptance in Me.

Love,
Your Daddy in heaven

Am I now trying to win the approval of men, or of God? Or am I trying to please men? If I were still trying to please men, I would not be a servant of Christ.

Galatians 1:10 NIV

7

The Lie

How do you feel about yourself after looking through a magazine filled with models? Have you ever noticed that these models never seem to look like us? And they have a look that we can't attain? Who are these models we long to look like? Their names don't really matter, because they're images of airbrushed perfection. What we see is not reality.

Every day we are bombarded with images of how we're supposed to look. One month thin is in; the next month round and curvy is the look. What about hair? Short, long, curly, bald . . . ? We see it, we want it!

It's hard to define who we really are and what we're supposed to look like with so many mixed signals flashing in our face. Even the models are mixed up and insecure. I have never met a model or pageant winner who has ever been completely happy with her appearance. So how is it possible that someone we've never even met influences us so powerfully? While perfecting our looks, we can lose sight of who we really are—awesome girls created in God's own image for a divine purpose.

It's time to change our idols to the things that really matter.

If God wrote a love letter to you . . .

My beautiful girl—

The world you live in is full of deception that will cause you confusion about who you are. This trap was set for My first daughter, Eve, and she fell for it. Deception is dangerous, and I want to protect you, My daughter, from a life wasted by living for yourself. Come to My Word and you will find wisdom to know the difference between right and wrong and between truth and lies. Carve My Truth into your character by living it, and let it become your guard, your guide, and your gauge to keep you from falling away from Me!

Love,
Your Daddy in heaven

Those people who make idols
are nothing themselves,
and the idols they treasure
are just as worthless.
Worshipers of idols are blind,
stupid, and foolish.

Isaiah 44:9 CEV

8

A Bad Hair Day

I always wanted big hair. Unfortunately, I was born with about ten pieces on my head. Several years ago I saw a commercial for clip-on hair extensions. I was so excited I bought tons of this clip-on hair. I looked like All-Hair-and-No-Face-Girl, but it didn't matter—I couldn't wait to go to my next speaking engagement with my new look.

At my speaking event, no one in the room of a thousand women had bigger hair than I had, and I imagine no one *wanted* to have bigger hair than I did that day. I went to the podium when it was time, and the lady who introduced me gave me a big old bear hug. Her embrace unclipped one of my spiffy new hair extensions, but I didn't know that.

I began my talk. I couldn't help noticing my audience seemed distracted. They were pointing and whispering to each other. So I stopped and said, "What are all you looking at?" The entire audience pointed to my feet. There my fake hair had fallen out all over the floor. I felt like God said to me: "The number of hairs on your head I know, but I don't recognize any of those!"

I still love big hair but have learned that no one cares how big my hair is but me. And God loves me just the way He made me.

If God wrote a love letter to you . . .

My beautiful girl—

I love what I have created. I am delighted in you! Don't ever feel insecure about what you think you are not, because I made you in My image. I did not give you such uniqueness, My love, for you to squeeze into a man-made mold. You are royalty, but you won't discover that truth by gazing into a mirror. Let Me be your mirror, and I will reflect back to you your true beauty. The more you gaze at Me, the more you will see My workmanship in you. The sooner you see yourself for who you really are, the sooner you can begin your reign as My priceless princess with a purpose.

Love,
Your Daddy in heaven

For we are God's masterpiece. He created us anew in Christ Jesus, so we can do the good things he planned for us long ago.

Ephesians 2:10

9

Beautiful Lips

I used to help find models and actors in Hollywood for movies, fashion magazines, and modeling agents. I traveled the country auditioning thousands and thousands of models, actors, and singers each year. As exciting as it was to watch these talented people get discovered, it was more exciting to see their lives changed by sharing with them God's power and purpose for their future!

In one talent search in Seattle, a group of gang members showed up to cause trouble. To be perfectly honest, I was scared, and I started praying for God to protect everyone. As I prayed, a very strange feeling impressed itself upon my heart. I felt that God wanted me to talk to those gang members.

At the moment, I was in a hotel lobby, protected by security, and the gang was right outside. Suddenly I could not stop myself from walking outside to them. I thought, *I'm either hearing from God, or I'm going to meet Him soon in heaven!*

I found the gang members and stood in front of them. Out of my mouth came the words, "God has a great plan for your life. Don't blow it. You have a future."

Their leader yelled back to me, "How would you know that, Barbie?"

"I know it because it's true," I said, and I invited them to audition for acting.

Every day of that week I was determined to use my lips to speak words of life to them. By the end of the week, the two gang members who were brothers came to my husband and me and asked us to pray with them. They told us that when they were only seven and eight years old, their parents pushed the boys out of the car and drove away. The boys had been placed in many different foster homes, most of them abusive. These young men were now eighteen and nineteen years old and didn't know what to do with their lives. But they wanted to change—and they DID!

To those gang members, my husband and I had more beautiful lips than any of the most attractive models we auditioned—because our lips spoke God's words of hope, love, and direction.

If God wrote a love letter to you . . .

My beautiful girl—

Did you know that I can give you beautiful lips with words of love, hope, and encouragement? I've anointed your lips to become irresistible to anyone who hears you speak! I want you to speak life to a lifeless world. While others use their lips to spread worthless words, you, My Princess, have the privilege of empowering people to make life-changing choices. Come to Me in prayer every day, and I will line your lips with love, wisdom, and encouragement for all who hear you speak.

Love,
Your Daddy in heaven

The tongue has the power of life and death.

Proverbs 18:21 GW

10

Prince Running Back

When I was in high school, I was running slow laps around the track one day like a wimp. I heard someone yell from the back of the bleachers, "Pick up your knees and run faster!" I looked over to see a typical "jock," a very handsome, dark-haired guy I knew was on the football team.

He yelled again, but I didn't realize he was yelling at me—good-looking boys had never noticed me before, so I ignored him. Then he ran down on the track beside me and said, "Didn't you hear me? Get your knees up and run faster!"

"Why should I?" I asked him.

"Because you need to run harder if you're going to be the next Miss USA," he shot back at me.

"What makes you think I want to be Miss USA?" I asked.

"Last year when you were weighing in at the health club, I was standing in line right behind you," he told me. "I heard you tell the manager your goals."

Now I was embarrassed, so I answered, "I was only kidding. I could never be Miss USA."

"I've watched you," he told me. "I've seen you get off drugs and lose all that weight. I think you can do anything. I'm proud of you."

I started to cry tears of joy, because no one other than my dad and stepmom had ever been proud of me or believed in me. I found out that this running back's name was Mark, but from that day on, I called him Prince Running Back. After he finished running with me, he offered to train me for the pageant. "What pageant?" I asked.

"The one I'm entering you in next year," he replied. I thought I must be dreaming. Someone had seen the best in me even before I had become the best version of me. But Prince Running Back taught me to believe that I could do anything if I would change the way I looked at myself and the world around me.

Ask God to open your eyes to how He sees you, and then let your Daddy in heaven change the way you see yourself and others.

If God wrote a love letter to you . . .

47

My beautiful girl—

I see greatness in you. Don't be afraid to dream big just because of past disappointments. Remember, it wasn't your faith in *Me* that failed you, it was your faith in people that caused the pain of broken dreams. I can do anything you ask in My name. King David started out as a small shepherd boy, but had faith big enough to kill a giant. I am just as real today in *you* as I was for David back then. So ask Me, obey Me, and seek Me with all your heart, mind, and strength. And then watch My promises to you come to pass in My perfect time.

Love,
Your Daddy in heaven

God can do anything, you know—far more than you could ever imagine or guess or request in your wildest dreams!

Ephesians 3:20 Message

11

We All Fall Down

I was competing in my first beauty pageant. As I'm sure you know, a huge part of every pageant is when the contestants do the walk with the wave, parading one at a time down the runway toward the audience. The runway and stage were lined with tiny little lights, and spotlights followed each contestant as she walked down the runway in her beautiful evening gown, as if she were a movie star. I had dreamed about this moment since the time I was a little girl, and now it was my turn.

I walked excitedly down the runway toward the light beaming in my face. Yet I managed to smile and wave. I took one step after another until there was nothing left to step on. Literally. I walked on air for a brief moment and then went flying off the end of the runway. I landed smack in the middle of the judges' table.

The audience gasped. Have you ever noticed that whenever you do something embarrassing, it seems like the whole world is there to witness it? Well, that was certainly my most embarrassing moment. I rolled off the table onto the floor, and the thought came to me, *I still want to win.* I mustered up the perkiest smile I could, crawled back up on the stage, looked at the judges, and said, "I just wanted you to remember me!" They did, and I won the pageant.

We all fall down at some time in life (maybe not off a stage), and we all want to win—and we can. It's not only how we act; it's how we react that makes us a winner. Not matter what you have done or what has been done to you, in God's strength you can and will finish this life a winner.

If God wrote a love letter to you . . .

My beautiful girl—

I am your loving Father. I will pick you up whenever you fall and set your feet on solid ground. All My chosen ones had to get up and receive My gift of grace to finish living out their faith. I gave My disciple Peter the strength to get up from the guilt. I gave My anointed king David the grace to get up from the shame of committing adultery. I gave My apostle Paul the mercy to get up from pride and arrogance. I gave My warrior Gideon the courage to get up from his fears. The time is now, My girl. Get up and finish what I called you to do. Nothing can keep you down, because My power to rise again is in you.

Love,
Your Daddy in heaven

The godly may trip seven times, but they will get up again.

Proverbs 24:16

12

My Clothes Revealed Me

When I lost all that weight while I was a senior in high school, I was so excited. I couldn't wait to wear miniskirts, tightly cropped tops, and backless dresses. I had worked hard on my body, so why shouldn't I show it off? Besides, all my friends dressed in sexy clothes, and I loved the way boys noticed me when I wore those kinds of clothes. I never thought much more about it until I overheard some boys talking about our homecoming queen, a girl named Sarah. One boy said, "Sarah is so awesome. She is just the kind of girl I want to marry someday."

Sarah was the only popular girl at our school who never showed her belly button, back, or breasts, or wore shorts that exposed her buns. So I couldn't resist asking, "Why would you marry someone like that? She is so conservative, and she dresses like a dork!"

To my surprise, the best-looking guy at school said, "She is a class act. She's the kind of girl you want to be the mother of your children. The other girls are only good for one thing."

"What's that?" I asked.

"Sex," he answered. "That's why they dress like prostitutes."

I was in shock. Sarah had good girlfriends and the respect and adoration of even the most popular boys at our school. She dared to be different and to keep her body covered even though she was in great physical shape. She wasn't hung up on how she dressed. Her clothes were cute but never sexy. I decided that I wanted the boys to look at me as a "class act" too. I wanted to be someone they would want to marry someday. Soon I learned it was more fun to be different. I liked being the leader in a new fashion trend, and best of all, people began treating me with respect and importance.

How about you? What message does your wardrobe give about who you are? Do your friends tell you what to wear? Are you a copycat or a class act? Go through your wardrobe today and get rid of everything that lowers the standard of who you really are. Let your wardrobe express that you are God's "awesome" girl.

If God wrote a love letter to you . . .

55

My beautiful girl—

You don't have to conform to the wardrobes of this world to feel good about yourself, My Princess. Remember, what you wear initially defines what people think about you. I want your wardrobe to honor Me. You don't need to dress to get attention—I can make you more beautiful than any fashion designer, because I specialize in internal and eternal makeovers. Your favor and beauty will radiate because you are a reflection of Me. Keep in mind that those who design clothes to expose your body do not love your soul like I do. Let your wardrobe reveal My Spirit—not your flesh. Robe yourself today like the royalty you are.

Love,
Your Daddy in heaven

Charm can be deceiving
and beauty fades away,
but a woman
who honors the Lord
deserves to be praised.

Proverbs 31:30 CEV

13

True Beauty

When I lived in Arizona, I met a group of young girls who wanted me to help them start a volunteer team that could get involved in community projects. These girls were beautiful—but more than that, they were in the winner's circle because their hearts wanted to make a difference.

We came up with a plan of action. We met with several charities like Feed the Children, Teen Challenge, Help the Homeless, Special Olympics, children's hospitals, and others. Not all of them were receptive to our help, but some were. We printed T-shirts with our team name: "Arizona USA." We hooked up a voicemail hotline so girls on the team could call in and find out what was going on in the community. Charities, churches, and ministries could also reach us if they needed the help of our team.

Eventually the community began taking us seriously. We started with ten girls, and within one year we had more than 150 girls on the team. Almost every weekend we were scheduled for some event—singing at a children's hospital or retirement home, helping to organize a fundraiser, working with the Special Olympics events, or visiting children's orphanages to play with the kids or lead them in special activities. But even greater than giving to our community was being able to watch the girls discover they were leaving beauty marks on people's hearts by being willing to help others.

Write down something you want to do to make a difference. Consider these possibilities: volunteer at a church by helping in the nursery; call your local charities or online ministries and ask how you can help; babysit for a single mom; listen to a friend; bring flowers to someone elderly and alone in a retirement home; create a website for troubled teens; head up a fundraiser for something or someone in need. There is nothing more beautiful than a girl who loves God with all her heart.

Be that girl!

If God wrote a love letter to you . . .

My beautiful girl—

I know there is a hero hidden in your heart whether you believe it or not. I know this because I am the One who placed a desire in your soul to conquer something great. The only thing holding you back from making a difference is you! Your generation needs you to live every day with courage. I don't want My girl hiding behind fears and insecurities or paralyzed by what people think anymore. You are My Princess Warrior, born to lead with your life, and I am your faithful Father, here to give you the courage to step out in faith. Do what is right, and don't be afraid; I am with you always, fighting for you every day!

Love,
Your Daddy in heaven

So be strong and courageous! Do not be afraid and do not panic before them. For the LORD your God will personally go ahead of you. He will neither fail you nor abandon you.

Deuteronomy 31:6

14

The Movie of Life Stars You

When I was in high school, I thought everyone was better than I was. I did not do as well as my friends in school because I had a learning disorder called *dyslexia*. Dyslexia causes you to see things backward, so if you have trouble understanding anything in this book, read it backward! I didn't have the talent to sing. I tried dance class once but was too uncoordinated. As a matter of fact, when I was on NBC's national live telecast of the Miss USA pageant, the choreographer decided to sit me on the piano bench for the opening dance number because I couldn't keep up during rehearsals, which caused the other girls to trip over me! When I graduated from high school, I had no idea what I was going to be when I grew up. I tried waiting tables, but on my first day on the job, I accidentally dumped a spinach salad on a bald man's head. I laughed and got fired on the spot.

There were only two things I did well—talk and make people laugh. But I did not realize that my obsession with talking to any poor soul within five feet of my reach could be considered a talent, nor did I ever think God could use my ability to help people laugh as a talent to heal hurting hearts. Today I'm still amazed that I get to do what I love— travel, meet people, and talk at conferences, churches, and retreats.

In the same way that God gave me a part in His Theater, He has a part for you to play. God's character acted out through you is the real Oscar, a trophy worth winning, because it's a powerful performance that changes people's lives. So keep practicing your talent, and memorize your lines in the Script (the Bible). If you take your role in God's movie of life seriously, you will be the spotlight in someone's darkness.

Play your part every day so that when the Producer calls, you will be ready.

If God wrote a love letter to you . . .

My beautiful girl—

I have given you the gift of eternal life, but My giving does not stop there. Inside of you is a supernatural surprise—a gift that is waiting to be unwrapped . . . by you. Yes, it's there. It's hidden behind dreams waiting to be pursued. Don't allow your dreams to be swallowed up by daily distractions and drowned by disappointment. Let Me help you clear out the clutter and find your gift. You'll find it in that place in your life that brings you the greatest joy, that place where your soul longs to be, that work your hands love to do. But this gift that I've given to you is not just for you. I have blessed you to be a blessing to others. When you find your gift, I will take it and multiply it beyond what you could ever imagine. So ask Me, and I will help you open your gift so that you can give it away to the world—not to impress, but to bless.

Love,
Your Daddy in heaven

Each of you has been blessed with one of God's many wonderful gifts to be used in the service of others. So use your gift well.

1 Peter 4:10 CEV

15

Relational Rides

If you are anything like me, you love amusement parks. I love the attractions, the wild rides, and of course, the food! Girlfriends are kind of like an amusement park experience. Friends can be fun, exciting, exhausting, overwhelming—all like a wild ride. Sometimes we forget how to ride our relationships the right way. Let me take you to *Girlfriendland* for an adventure together, through some main attractions that may change the way you see your girlfriends and yourself.

Our first stop is the Relational Roller Coaster. This ride will make you laugh and scream and, of course, turn you upside down. Before you get in line for the ride, I need you to read the following:

R—Ride with care.

U—Understand that we all react differently to the ride.

L—Learn from each other's reactions.

E—Expect more from yourself than from your friends.

S—Stay close during the ups and downs.

Let's get in line together and wait our turn to take what will be one of the most important rides of our lives. If you have experienced being a friend, you've found out that it is a lot of work. But it's worth the ticket price to learn how to ride out our differences.

Sometimes we get on the ride with great anticipation for how fun and exciting our new friend will be. But many times we discover that the twists and turns are more than we can handle, and we feel a little sick or scared. Just like on a real roller coaster, we need to be ready for the ride. I've had a lot of great girlfriends whom I love and cherish, but not one of my friendships has been a smooth ride. It takes time to learn how to respond to, relate to, and respect the Relational Roller Coaster.

Real friends are worth the time!

If God wrote a love letter to you . . .

My beautiful girl—

You are of great value to My Kingdom and Me. Because of the great call I have placed on your life, I want you to be cautious who you allow in your circle of friends. I want My girl to surround herself with people who complete you . . . not deplete you. Friends who build you up, not tear you down. Yes, I want you to love everyone, but love Me enough to choose friends who draw you closer to Me and help you conquer your calling. If you will ask Me, I will assign divine friendships to you just as I gave My chosen king David his best friend Jonathan.

Love,
Your Daddy in heaven

There are "friends" who destroy each other, but a real friend sticks closer than a brother.

Proverbs 18:24

16

Friends

Relationships are only fun and fulfilling if we really care for each other. It is not enough to merely say you care. You need to back your words up with your actions. Do you really care about your relationships, or are you in it for a free ride? Take the Friendship Quiz below and find out.

1. My friend is stressed out about passing a final test, so I . . .
   a. invite her to come over and help her study, then call the next day to find out how she did.
   b. tell her not to worry, then talk her into blowing it off and going out.
2. My friend is bummed out about her weight, so I . . .

a. tell her she's beautiful no matter what she weighs, then offer to diet and exercise with her for the next month.

b. tell her to stop weighing herself and to throw out the scale.

3. My friend has to do a bunch of chores before we can go out to the mall, so I . . .

a. offer to come over and help so we can go together.

b. tell her I'll meet her at the mall because I don't want to wait.

Now let's look at your answers:

All A's

You are the "real deal." You are someone who truly cares about the relational ride. Your friends are blessed to ride with you. Keep up the "heart" work!

Any B's

If you answered any of the B's, you will not enjoy the Relational Roller Coaster because you don't care with your actions. Anyone can say they care, but a real friend shows it. So get back in line and ride with care.

We all need help when it comes to being a good friend. I have found if I go into the friendship for what I can give and not what I can get, I become the kind of friend I want to have.

If God wrote a love letter to you . . .

My beautiful girl—

I want you to become the kind of friend you want to have. Follow your Father in heaven and love your friends and family without any expectations. Let Me define for you what a true and healthy relationship is. If you will ask Me, I will help you become a good friend who brings glory to Me. You have My Spirit inside of you; therefore, you have the power in you to love others the most when they deserve it the least . . . the way I love you! Remember this, My daughter, you represent heaven above by the way you love.

Love,
Your Daddy in heaven

A friend is always loyal,
and a brother is born to help in time of
need.

Proverbs 17:17

17

Divinely Different

I used to think that if my friends were not smiling and laughing 24/7, they must not want to ride the relational roller coaster with me. That's not true. We all react differently by God's design.

If we put Tanya Talker on the roller coaster, she talks to everyone waiting in line with her. Even if they don't want to talk, they have to listen, because she's laughing as loud as she talks. She approaches this ride with excitement. Next in line is Deanna Doer. She pushes people out of the way to get to the front car because it's the most adventurous place on the ride. She puts her hands up the whole time. She likes the thrill of not hanging onto anything, as opposed to Tanya, who hangs on to the poor person's head in front of her. Now Thoughtful Theresa observes the ride to make sure it's safe. She checks out who will be riding with her, and she quietly times how long the ride takes. Last but not least, Patient Paula is in no hurry. She watches everyone riding the ride before her and enjoys their reactions.

All of us enjoy the roller coaster in different ways, and we all react differently to the ups and downs and twists and turns. *Different* doesn't mean we can't ride together. I've learned from watching Deanna Doer that I need to work before I play, and I've learned from Thoughtful Theresa how to organize my schedule and to think before I speak. My best friends are Patient Paulas, and they have taught me to be a better listener. Your friends are put on your relational ride with you for a reason. Don't miss out on the excitement of growing together.

And remember to sometimes take a seat next to someone who needs a friend as much as you do.

If God wrote a love letter to you . . .

My beautiful girl—

I created each person with a different blueprint. None of My chosen children are exactly alike. I am a God who knows how to color the world around you with every kind of creation. I share this with you so you will not waste your years trying to become someone or something you were not meant to be. I am asking you as your heavenly Father to respect yourself and others. Don't get trapped into playing the self-defeating game of comparison. Embrace who you are and how distinctive others are. Don't allow the uniqueness I created in each person to cause division. Break down the walls and be the one who accepts and respects each person for who I made them to be!

Love,
Your Daddy in heaven

God works in different ways, but it is the same
God who does the work in all of us.

1 Corinthians 12:6

18

Gabby Go-karts

Words matter. Our words are like go-karts—gabby ones. Ever see the movie *Cars*? Picture yourself as a talking go-kart on a racetrack with car friends lined up next to you. How you race around that track affects how your friends will see you. Do you weave all over the track, jabbering all sorts of trash-talk, crashing your relationships on the course as you bulldoze your way to the finish line? Or are you driving your best and encouraging your friends to do the same, cheering them on, as someone who will win your friends' hearts while racing the track? Think about this:

R—Race to win friends with your mouth.

U—Understand how to keep your tongue on the right track.

L—Learn when to stop talking.

E—Eliminate gossip from your conversations.

S—Say the right thing.

Our Gabby Go-karts can draw people to us or cause people to hide so they won't have to ride with us. Don't waste your words by trying to prove your point, get your way, talk out of turn, or bring bad news.

Have you ever met someone who caused you to cringe every time they talked? I have. It was a girl at our school who was on the cheerleading team. When she was in front of an audience, she had lots of energy and a big smile, and she yelled victory cheers enthusiastically. But when the game was over, Little Miss Cheerleader turned into Big Miss Downer, and I'm not talking touchdowns. It did not matter what anyone said, she always had something bad or depressing to say to the group. Eventually people started to avoid her. One day I saw her sobbing in the bathroom. I asked her how I could help. "Find me some friends who are not so negative and mean!" she told me. I could not believe that she could not see how her own lips were making her lose friends.

If you want to know how well you race with your mouth, then pay attention to how people respond to you after you talk. In other words, read the caution signs while you are running your mouth. Then slow down long enough to learn from the other drivers on your track.

That way, you'll win friends.

If God wrote a love letter to you . . .

My beautiful girl—

Did you know that I've anointed your lips with the power to speak life to a lifeless world? I love your mouth because it is Mine—ready to be filled with My words. While others are using their lips to spread worthless words, you, My Princess, have the privilege of changing people's perspectives and empowering them to make life-changing choices that will point them to Me. Your words are more valuable than priceless jewels. I want you to come to Me in prayer every day, and I will fill your mouth with love, wisdom, and encouragement. I will make your mouth and lips My masterpiece for all who hear you speak.

Love,
Your Daddy in heaven

And whatever you do or say, do it as a representative of the Lord Jesus.

Colossians 3:17

19

Share Your Faith

My best friend in high school watched me go through my parents' divorce, my drug problems, my boyfriend issues, and my eating disorder. But she never offered to pray me through my pain or invited me to church. When I asked her about it later, she said that she was afraid to talk to me about God. If only she had not been ashamed of God and His life-changing words in the Bible.

If you are a Christian, don't be scared or embarrassed to talk about God with others. People need help finding their way. Look around you. Very few people will reject prayer. I'm not saying you have to start a student crusade on campus, but you can offer to pray for people when they need help and invite them to church. I know it seems hard to speak out, but if you will tenderly offer to pray for a friend when she is hurting, she will get to see how real God is by the way you love her and live out your faith in front of her. God will give you the words even when you have no idea what to say.

Take the first step. Your Father in heaven will give you supernatural courage to help you walk out your faith in front of your friends.

My beautiful girl—

I know you are surrounded by broken families and brokenhearted friends. I see your hurting heart for the world you live in. I want to give you the tools to rebuild broken hearts with words of hope and rebuild broken relationships with forgiveness and grace. If you are willing to reach out, then I will go before you and prepare the hearts of your friends. If you are willing, I will do more than you could ever dream. Together we will help many find their way to heaven's door.

Love,
Your Daddy in heaven

But now I said to them, "You know very well what trouble we are in. Jerusalem lies in ruins, and its gates have been destroyed by fire. Let us rebuild the wall of Jerusalem and end this disgrace!"

Nehemiah 2:17

20

Gossip

Gossip is not the same as just gabbing. Gossip is sharing information that hurts someone's reputation or causes others to think badly about the person you're gossiping about. If one of your friends gossips to you about others, I can guarantee they will gossip about you. Take a minute to think about how you feel about yourself after you race your mouth with harmful words and comments. You feel like you've fallen off the track, because no one likes a gossip. They may listen to your trash, but they won't help you pick it up. Before you share personal or inaccurate information about another person, ask yourself the following questions:

1. Why am I sharing this information?
2. How will it benefit the person listening?
3. Am I willing to let my name be used as a reference when someone repeats what I'm sharing?
4. How would the person feel if she were standing next to me while I was gossiping about her?

If your answers to any of the questions are not positive ones, change direction. Don't gossip and get off track. Nothing will make a friendship blow up faster than gossip, so get a tune-up on your tongue. And when someone gossips about you, don't get even by getting ugly. Your true character will eventually win the race against your reputation.

Remember, even if the gossip is true, it's the wrong way to go.

If God wrote a love letter to you . . .

My beautiful girl—

Every day you will be faced with the opportunity to talk about others. But I'm asking you to let Me take control of your conversations. When you are tempted to give in to gossip, pray. I'm the only One who can tame your tongue. Talk to Me. I know how hard it is to think before you speak, but I will help you. I want you to be careful who you listen to and what conversations you engage in. Socializing with the wrong people and getting involved with useless conversation or harmful hearsay can cost you friendships and even your reputation. I am willing to listen to all that concerns you about others. So talk to Me first, and I will give you words of wisdom in how to build up others and glorify Me.

Love,
Your Daddy in heaven

Mean people spread mean gossip;
their words smart and burn.
Troublemakers start fights;
gossips break up friendships.

Proverbs 16:27–28 Message

21

The Argue Arcade

Most of us don't really want to argue, but anger happens. So many friends and families argue away their love for each other. So how do we play the game in the Argue Arcade? Let's start with the rules:

R—Refuse to lose it.
U—Unfinished fights don't fix it.
L—Learn to let go and forgive.
E—Excuses don't win a prize.
S—Say you're sorry.

My dad used to say to me, "Don't win the battle and lose the war." Those are winning words to live by. Who cares about winning a small battle if a big major war is lost? The best way to win is to let the other person do the dirty fighting. Keep yourself clean. Winners stop arguments before they begin. How do you do that? Believe me, there is a way to win your argument without losing your friends:

1. Listen to what the other person has to say before you jump in the ring with your boxing gloves on.
2. Thank the person for being truthful.
3. Pray for the person to hear your heart and for words of wisdom.
4. Remember that you can say anything if you learn to say it with the right attitude.
5. If you feel you're about to lose it, leave the Argue Arcade immediately, and don't return until you're ready to play fair.

When I'm upset and don't know what to do, I try not to do anything. So often we say and do something while we are upset that we regret later. It's better to swallow your angry words than to have to eat them later. And sometimes you will need to agree to disagree in order to finish a fight and save a friendship. Of course we all lose it sometimes, so don't be too hard on yourself or your friend when it happens. God does not expect us never to feel angry. But if you do lose it, go to your heavenly Father, confess your anger, and let Him deal with your heart so that you can make it right.

If God wrote a love letter to you . . .

My beautiful girl—

I know how hard it is to react the right way when feelings of anger and disappointment hit your heart. I, your Lord, have felt every emotion you feel when I walked the earth. I am not asking you not to feel anger, I am warning you not to give in to your anger and allow anyone to provoke you to compromise your character. Bitterness is the bait of Satan. If you bite his bait and internalize your anger, you will become bitter. Nothing good can be birthed out of bitterness. Come to Me—your Daddy in heaven—and pour out your angry heart. Only I can turn your anger into amazing grace for those who have caused you pain.

Love,
Your Daddy in heaven

Look after each other so that none of you fails to receive the grace of God. Watch out that no poisonous root of bitterness grows up to trouble you, corrupting many.

Hebrews 12:15

22

Forgiveness

Many things cause weeds to grow in our garden of life, and weeds kill our beautiful garden. When I lost all my weight, dropped sugar from my diet, and started exercising, my depression went away for a long time. However, it returned a few years later. I did not understand that, although I was eating healthy, exercising, praying, reading my Bible, and going to church, I still had some pesky weeds growing in my garden.

One weed was *unforgiveness*. I still did not forgive my mom for hurting me with her words or my dad for his temper or both of them for getting a divorce. These three weeds in my garden were working against my efforts to be the best version of me. So I wrote letters to both of my parents, telling them I loved them. Then I set some boundaries so I would no longer let them use words to hurt me. Once I did this, the weeds died and the roots of my depression were ripped out.

If someone has badly wounded you, you will be held captive to that hurt until you offer forgiveness to that individual. Forgiveness sets a prisoner free.

Once you forgive, you will realize that the prisoner was you.

If God wrote a love letter to you . . .

My beautiful girl—

Forgiveness is My gift to you. Now I want you to give this same gift away to those who have let you down or disappointed you. I know there are people who have done horrible things that seem unforgivable. But I am a just God, and you can trust Me to deal with those who have hurt My daughter. What I ask of you will unlock the door that holds your heart hostage in a prison of pain. You can't soar when you carry heavy chains of unforgiveness. I want to see My girl free and full of life. If you refuse to forgive, you are not only hurting those who have caused you pain, you are hurting yourself, My love. Please take the keys to freedom that I offer you to release yourself from this prison of pain, and forgive as I your Father have forgiven you.

Love,
Your Daddy in heaven

O Lord, you are so good, so ready to forgive,
so full of unfailing love for all who ask
for your help.

Psalm 86:5

23

Deal with Depression

What is depression? It's a hopeless, exhausted, I'm-not-having-fun, life-stinks, get-out-of-my-face, I-can't-deal-with-it, leave-me-alone, let-me-eat-chocolate state of mind. That just about sums it up.

Depression is attacking girls and women everywhere. The top-selling drug in our country is for depression. If you have some depressed days, don't worry—we all have them. It's easy to fall into that pit, and there are so many negative forces that hit our hearts. But when depressed days turn into weeks, and weeks turn into months, it's time to deal with depression.

Whenever I feel depressed, I cry out to God. I mean, I actually tell Him that I hate life right at that moment. I tell Him that I have no hope or joy, so I need Him to roll the stone away from my hurting heart and give me back my purpose, power, and peace.

After I am done crying to my Daddy in heaven, I ask Him to show me who I can encourage or help. You will be amazed at how a prayer for help and helping someone else will give you a vacation from your own problems.

God has a purpose for pain—and one purpose is to enable you to help someone else through your shared experiences. Paul reminds us, "He [God] comforts us when we are in trouble, so that we can share that same comfort with others in trouble" (2 Cor. 1:4 CEV).

Take a moment right now and pray for a way to make someone else's day.

If God wrote a love letter to you . . .

My beautiful girl—

I hear your heartfelt tears from heaven. Never forget that I am here for you in the dark hours of the night, My daughter. When you are in need of a daddy to hold you, I will reach for you and you will feel My Spirit uplifting you. When you pour your heart out to Me, I will wash away the pain that is keeping you down. My mighty hand will wipe away every tear you have cried, and not a single drop will be wasted. I know what you need, and your tears will be turned into joy very soon.

Love,
Your Daddy in heaven

But in my distress I cried out to the Lord;
   yes, I prayed to my God for help.
He heard me from his sanctuary;
   my cry to him reached his ears.

Psalm 18:6

24

Friends Are Like Elevator Buttons

Friends are like buttons on an elevator—they can take you up or bring you down. If you don't surround yourself with friends who bring you up, you will become like those friends who bring you down.

I was moved around a lot when I was a child. By the time I was in high school, I had attended six different schools. So I was desperate for friends. I never gave a thought to who those friends were or what they acted like. I just wanted to be liked by somebody.

Unfortunately, I began hanging out with the "it's-cool-to-be-crude" crowd. Within one year after I joined this crowd, I started being rude to my dad and my stepmom. I started swearing, smoking, and getting stoned every day before school. I gained weight, started dressing like an "I-don't-care" slob, and my happy heart turned into a hard heart. The weird thing was that I did not notice how much I had changed until one bad choice after another turned me into someone I did not want to be. It was a dangerous drug overdose that gave me the wake-up call to make better choices in my life. And that included choosing better friends.

I want to challenge you to take a moment and write down the names of your friends on a piece of paper. Then write down how you would describe them and how you feel about yourself when you're with them. Next, invite someone you trust to tell you honestly what he or she thinks about your choices for friends. Don't get defensive when that person gives you the answers—just listen and learn. Don't take chances just to please your friends. One wrong experience at the wrong time can unplug your power to win what you really want out of life.

If God wrote a love letter to you . . .

My beautiful girl—

You never have to compromise your character to feel loved and accepted. Self-respect is a mark of honor. Anyone can follow the crowd, but you are not just anyone—you are Mine. I will give you the strength to conquer compromise. I know you feel a pull in your heart every day to give in to peer pressure. There is a war for your life and even your soul, My beloved daughter, and temptation is a test of your faith that only I can help you pass. Turn to Me in prayer and trust that I know what is best for My girl. Don't give in to temptation and don't give up the fight to do what is right. I promise I will carry you through. I'll not let any wicked winds blow out the flame of your faith.

Love,
Your Daddy in heaven

They do not compromise with evil,
and they walk only in his paths.
You have charged us
to keep your commandments carefully.

25

A Ride on the Wild Side

During my senior year of high school, our beautiful homecoming queen decided to walk on the wild side on homecoming night. Before that night, she never drank, smoked, or went to the wrong parties. But on this night our homecoming king talked her into experiencing life on the edge. She chose to drink along with him and their other friends on the homecoming court. She discovered that she liked the feeling of being tipsy from a little alcohol, so she drank even more that evening, and so did he.

While our king was driving our queen to their homecoming celebration—both of them a little drunk—he swerved onto the wrong side of the road. Their car hit another car carrying a mother and her young children head-on at fifty miles per hour. The young family was killed, and the homecoming queen, who was not wearing a seat belt, flew through the windshield. She did not die, but she was cut up and scarred severely all over her face and body. To this day she walks with a cane.

It's not worth "just one time." There are countless stories about young people like her who would give anything to get another chance to make the right choice.

Pray before you make any choice, and let God direct your steps.

If God wrote a love letter to you . . .

My beautiful girl—

There will always be two roads before you, My love. The popular road is easy, and its bumps are worn smooth by the wandering crowds. This road appears safe simply because so many have already ventured around its curves and shuffled down into its valleys. What the crowds don't understand is that this road is filled with regret and guilt, and it ultimately leads to death. This is the road that leads away from Me. If you find yourself on the wrong path, please cry out to Me. I will help you find your way and lead you back to the road that leads to life again—the road your feet were created to walk on. Throughout My Word, you will find signposts that will give you wisdom and direction. So keep reading and walking, My Princess, and you will begin to discover the real joy of the journey of life.

Love,
Your Daddy in heaven

Be careful to obey all these commands I am giving you. Show love to the Lord your God by walking in his ways and holding tightly to him.

Deuteronomy 11:22

26

Safe Sex ... What's That?

My father always told me that the way to get a guy to treat you like a princess is to act like one. Among other things, that meant I should be pure. His wise words worked for a while. But all my friends were playing the game of sex, and it seemed like they enjoyed themselves. I felt like I was missing out by refusing to play. Temptation, curiosity, and peer pressure won, and so I decided to check into the Impurity Zone with my boyfriend, who I really thought I loved.

Before that night, my boyfriend and I had a great relationship. We loved hanging out together, and he treated me with respect. But the day after we stepped over the line, he acted differently toward me. He wasn't just different; he was distant. I didn't feel like his princess anymore. I felt dethroned from my special place in his heart.

The Safe Sex Team teaches players how to protect themselves while they play around. Unfortunately, however, there is nothing to protect the players' hearts from getting hurt when they give in to the game of Safe Sex. The coaches of the Safe Sex Team mess with the minds of their players. They bend so many of God's great rules about sex that the team does not know how to play by the rules any longer. These players lose more than the game. They lose their self-respect. Even if a girl player tackles a boy's heart with her "safe sex" game tactics, she doesn't know how to hold on to it. So many times, that boyfriend trades that girl off for some new girl player.

After my first play in the Impurity Zone, I wanted to rewind that night so badly, but I couldn't because I was pregnant. When my boyfriend found out, he walked off the field and quit the game of love with me. Not only was I nauseous, emotional, and scared out of my mind, I was totally paralyzed by the pain of playing the sex game.

What team do you want to play on? It's a very serious game.

If God wrote a love letter to you . . .

My beautiful girl—

Your body is a gift from Me, and you are too valuable to let the wrong person open that gift. You are My treasure, and My Spirit dwells within you. I know there is an inner war raging for your soul and your body, and it fights against all you know to be true. Remember, My love, I can fight this battle for you, so don't compromise My best for you for a moment of passion. I know it may seem harmless to give yourself away, but the pain is not worth the pleasure. You are a princess too valuable to give yourself away. Give your whole heart to Me, and I will express My love to you in ways that will fill your heart. While you wait, I am preparing your husband to love you as the treasure you are!

Love,
Your Daddy in heaven

Run from sexual sin! No other sin so clearly affects the body as this one does. For sexual immorality is a sin against your own body.

27

It's a Life... Not a Choice

When I realized I was pregnant back in high school, I visited Planned Parenthood. I hoped they could give me some comfort and coaching. In the waiting room were ten other pregnant teenagers. I didn't know their stories, but clearly we were all left alone and injured from playing in the game of sex.

The nurse at Planned Parenthood walked in just as I was replaying in my mind: *One night equals this mess!* She handed each of us a pill to relax us. Before I took the pill, I asked, "Is this baby alive inside of me?"

"Of course not," she told me. "It's just a growth until five months."

With that answer I took the pill and thirty minutes later I was rolled into a room for the doctor to remove the "growth." As soon as I left that place, I knew in my heart that I had made another bad play. I had lost my virginity, my boyfriend, and now a baby. I was desperate to stop thinking and replaying my poor choices in my mind. So I tried to kill my memory with drugs.

Maybe you won't get stuck in the same bad position from your first play as I did. But you will lose your ability to win what you really want—a real relationship with a boy who loves you for all the right reasons. I know I'm hitting you hard, but I want you to do more than play safe. Not only do I want to block you from giving your body and soul to the wrong guy at the wrong time, I want you to win.

So if I have to be the one to tackle you with the truth, I will. I'm a coach who really cares!

If God wrote a love letter to you . . .

My beautiful girl—

No matter where you go or what you have done, I want you to know that I have covered you. I don't want My girl carrying guilt or shame. I cover your shame and give you a new life to shine for Me. I cover your guilt and give you grace. I wrap you in My arms and say you are My pure and beautiful daughter. When you ask Me, your heavenly Father, to forgive you, I cast your sins into the sea of forgetfulness and remember them no more. You are free, My Princess. Now embrace your new life and soar!

Love,
Your Daddy in heaven

Fear not; you will no longer live in shame.
    Don't be afraid; there is no more dis-
    grace for you.
You will no longer remember the shame of
    your youth.

28

The Music of Your Heart

I love music. I have it on all the time. It speaks to my soul. Music can be the magic that motivates you to excellence. It can inspire you and make you happy. Music can also cause you to think about sex, death, and other sad things.

The power of music reminds me that we should guard our hearts. Guard who you are and what you are becoming. Take a moment to write down or read out loud the lyrics of your favorite songs, without the music. If the words send messages that you don't agree with, don't listen any longer. You're too awesome to be brainwashed into becoming a broken girl.

You don't have to put on a blindfold to guard your mind. All you have to do is to dump the junk in your life that makes your head swim with confusion and causes your dreams to die. What we listen to will control what we think.

When I was involved in beauty pageants, all I read were beauty magazines. Eventually those beauty magazines and their articles about beauty and boys consumed my mind. All I ever thought about was my body and my beauty. Sadly, my mind's obsession with body and beauty made me a bulimic for many years. Today I don't waste my time reading anything that wastes my mind.

You will never regret guarding your greatest power—your power to be smart. So lifeguard your heart!

If God wrote a love letter to you . . .

My beautiful girl—

I want to protect you, but I will never force you to obey Me. I created your mind to dwell on what is true, pure, and right, but the choice is yours, My beloved daughter. If you'll cautiously consider what you watch, read, and listen to, you will keep your faith and find purpose for living. Pray, and I will point out to you the things that can carry you away from your calling and destroy your dedication to Me. I have destined you to live a life of influence for others to follow; this life is yours for the asking. I will continue to call to you to guard your heart and mind so you can experience the blessed life I have to offer to you . . . My daughter!

Love,
Your Daddy in heaven

Finally, brothers, whatever is true, whatever is noble, whatever is right, whatever is pure, whatever is lovely, whatever is admirable—if anything is excellent or praiseworthy—think about such things.

Philippians 4:8 NIV

29

Love Is a Gift

When I was in my teens and early twenties, I was in love with love. I never cared who the boy was as long as he made all the right moves and said all the right things. Using my heart without using my head left me broken most of the time in my young love life.

Maybe you're the same. Do you throw your heart down the field hoping any player will catch it? That's dangerous. Your heart is your most valuable piece of playing equipment in this game. Guard it by giving attention to how you play. Use your head—and don't hold your heart out for anyone to steal. When I learned how to handle my heart, I won self-respect. I won self-control. And I won back my confidence.

I love to feel like a winner. I love to hear the cheers for my choices. That does not mean I never experience some rough plays. But I've learned that if you keep your head in the game instead of playing games, you discover love is a gift and not a game. In the next devotion we will learn the rules of love that will win you what you really want: love, honor, and respect from a man of God who will one day walk you down the aisle and love you for the beautiful princess you are!

If God wrote a love letter to you . . .

My beautiful girl—

You are a gift, and your heart is priceless. Who do you hand your heart to? Do they draw you closer to Me, or do they weaken your faith in Me and draw you away? I gave My life so you could be free from being desperate for love. I don't want you to play relational games to get attention. You have the full attention of heaven because I am your Father. I know what's right for My daughter. Hold on to Me and let go of those who harm you. Then you'll be free from their power, and you'll see clearly what a real, lasting relationship is meant to be.

Love,
Your Daddy in heaven

Love is patient, love is kind. It does not envy,
it does not boast, it is not proud. It is not rude,
it is not self-seeking, it is not easily angered,
it keeps no record of wrongs.

1 Corinthians 13:4–5 NIV

30

Some Rules to Live By

When I say the "rules," I don't mean games to get a guy; I mean rules that will make or break the success of any guy-girl relationship. As you get to know a guy and before you consider handing your heart to him:

1. *Set boundaries up front*: Make sure he knows your boundaries. Either he will respect your rules or he will walk away. If he walks, he wasn't the right one, and you saved yourself much heartache and wasted time.

2. *Invite your friends*: Ask your friends to hang out with you and the guy you like. This will help you see how he interacts with others. Ask your close friends if they saw any weird or negative attitudes or behaviors.

3. *Avoid being alone with him*: And if you want to spend time together, stay in public places and keep doors open. This will keep you in control of your convictions. You will also avoid the chance of date rape or doing something you'll regret.

4. *Don't intercept his play*: Let him call you; don't ever call him. Why would you put yourself in a position to feel rejected if he does not call back? Besides, if he has to call you, he will hang on to your every word when he does reach you on the phone. Today's girls are stealing their guys' position of pursuing!

5. *Don't let him kiss you until you know his character, his friends, his family, and his intentions*: There is something so irresistible to a guy when a girl refuses to give in. I did not kiss my husband until he proposed to me, and it was the most romantic kiss I've ever experienced. It was worth the wait! I'm not saying don't kiss until you're engaged, but wait for a winner.

6. *Get a close-up shot on how he treats women*: Watch how he treats his own mother and sisters, because that's how he will eventually treat you.

7. *Pray hard*: Even better yet, have him pray with you. If he won't pray, he is not for you. You need a winner who knows how to pray with you.

There you have it—seven winning rules that will help you find the gift of real love!

If God wrote a love letter to you . . .

My beautiful girl—

I will always come when you call for Me, My love. I am your Daddy in heaven, and I want you to come to Me anytime you wish. I am always available to My girl, so call out to Me as many times as you need Me and I will come comfort you. I never tire of hearing your sweet voice speak My name. When your heart is broken, I want to put all the pieces back in place for you. When you feel empty, I will fill you up again and again. When your spirit has been crushed, My love, I am always available to you anytime you need Me. Call to Me and I will answer.

Love,
Your Daddy in heaven

The LORD hears his people when they call to him for help.

He rescues them from all their troubles.

The LORD is close to the brokenhearted; he rescues those whose spirits are crushed.

Psalm 34:17–18

31

The "Mr. Right" Checklist

Don't let a crush cancel out your checklist. Sometimes we get hit hard in the heart because the guy we like knows all the right moves, says all the right things, and, of course, is cute to the max. But is he truly Mr. Right? Are his motives in line with your checklist?

The "Mr. Right" Checklist

- Does he have his own faith in God?
- Does he go to church?
- Does he treat his mom and sister well?

- Does he bring out the best in you?
- Does he treat you like a princess (opens doors, talks with respect and honor to you and about you)?
- Does he pay for most dates?
- Does he make you feel important and valued?
- Does he honor your rules?
- Does he honor your parents' rules?
- Does he treat your parents with kindness?
- Does he have career and/or college goals?
- Does he have a clean mouth, even around his friends?
- Does he make you laugh?
- Do you feel happy when you are with him?
- Does he listen to you without interrupting or tuning you out?
- Does he seem like he would make a good husband and father?
- Will he pray with you?

I know this is a long list, but you are a girl who deserves the best. Don't waste your heart and time on a player who uses his looks and loves with his words only. Do whatever it takes to stay on the Pure Power team. It's worth the work, and it's worth the wait to win it all!

You deserve it!

If God wrote a love letter to you . . .

My beautiful girl—

There are no words to describe how much I love you. That is why I stretched out My arms of love and died for you. I know sometimes you don't feel lovable, but you don't have to earn My affection. I adore you. You are My creation. I never want you to doubt My commitment to you. I am the Lover of your soul, so let Me meet your every need. I long to set you free from searching for false love in the wrong places. Let Me hold on to your heart and fill you up with eternal love. Then you will feel My holy presence and fall in love with Me.

Love,
Your Daddy in heaven

May you experience the love of Christ, though it is too great to understand fully. Then you will be made complete with all the fullness of life and power that comes from God.

Ephesians 3:19

32

As White As Snow

I thought there was no way back to purity if you had already played the sex game. But while sitting in a small church during a Good Friday service, I heard a pastor say lovingly, "If any of you are holding on to a secret sin, you are stopping God from making you white as snow." This truth hit my heart, and I wanted to give my last secret sin to God that evening. But I was so ashamed of that secret—my abortion—that I had never confessed it to God for fear of His total disappointment.

God used that pastor to help me literally carry this burden to the cross. The church had set up a big wooden cross in the sanctuary, and everyone had been handed some paper and nails. The pastor gave us the opportunity to take any hidden sin to the cross and physically nail it there to be left forever.

That Friday I felt God's hand wipe away the last tear about the baby I had aborted. I know I will never feel good about my choice, but I can use the pain to serve as a warning to help those thinking about abortion. I can accept God's forgiveness and move on with my life. I look forward to holding that baby someday in heaven.

If you want to be pure again, pray this prayer with me now:

Dear God, I confess I have sinned sexually, and I'm sorry. I want Your plan for purity today. Please make me pure again in my mind, body, and spirit, I pray in Jesus' name. Amen.

If God wrote a love letter to you . . .

My beautiful girl—

Never fear, My chosen daughter, you are under My wing and covered with My Son's blood. The cross covered your guilt, I covered your shame, and you are covered with My extravagant love! As soon as you ask My forgiveness, I never again remember your wrongs. No matter what you have done or where you have gone, in My eyes you are now as white as snow. You are a pure princess in My sight—a new creation and covered by My grace and mercy forever. Now get up and enjoy the rest of your days, knowing you are covered, My beloved girl.

Love,
Your Daddy in heaven

Purify me from my sins, and I will be clean;
wash me, and I will be whiter than snow.

Psalm 51:7

33

Parent Talk

I grew up thinking I was in the wrong family because my parents were always fighting, screaming, and walking out on each other. They eventually divorced. When I was at my friends' homes, it appeared that they had the perfect families, while I lived in the haunted house. I was too young to understand either of these people called my parents. So I locked them out of my life with my actions and attitude.

Often I wanted to escape from my family or to run away. Looking back, I realize that if I had poured love and kindness into my hurting mom and dad, I may have helped my family instead of contributing to the destruction. I was so busy being mad at them for fighting that I forgot that I really did need them. I learned that life is hard, and although our families may be freaky, they are still the ones who stay by us regardless of the things we do.

When my parents divorced, it rocked *and* relieved my world. They were no longer fighting because they were no longer together. That was a relief. But we were no longer a family because we were apart. It may be that some parents are so paralyzed by pain that they pass it on to their children instead of giving God their problems to fix and grabbing on to the power He has to heal them. But we don't have to let their actions keep us in the dark.

Over the years I have learned that love conquers all. For many years I spent most of my time haunting my parents with the memories of their mistakes instead of cleaning out my own closet, which was filled with the cobwebs of a need to forgive. I knew I could not fix their marriage problems, but I wish I had helped to create a happy home instead of adding to the pain and problems.

If God wrote a love letter to you . . .

My beautiful girl—

Family is a gift from Me. But sadly, sometimes your greatest fight may be with your family. I want you to remember that no one is perfect. People will say things that hurt you or make you angry. When this happens, I want you to come to Me and pray—then I want you to forgive those who have hurt you just like I forgive you when you make mistakes. My precious girl, do not let anyone keep you from being kind and strong in your faith. Show love, honor, and respect to your parents, and I will bless you with special things I long to give you for obeying me.

Love,
Your Daddy in heaven

If it is possible, as far as it depends on you,
live at peace with everyone.

Romans 12:18 NIV

34

Moms

A young girl named Ann disliked everything about her mother. Every day she would avoid her mother like the plague, trying to think of ways to hurt her for all the things her mom had done and said to her.

One day she was telling her best friend, Barb, about her thoughts, and Barb came up with a great idea for revenge. The plan was for Ann to be the best daughter possible for six weeks. Ann was to do everything her mother said with a smile. She was not to argue or try to win her way. Every day Ann would tell her mother that she loved her. At the end of the six weeks, Ann's final revenge would be to crush her mother's heart by running away.

It was the perfect plan! After six weeks, Barb and Ann got together to plan the "runaway." Barb asked Ann if she had all of her belongings packed and ready to go. Finally Ann said, "I can't do it. Somehow, in these past six weeks I've learned to love my mom again. I want to stay home with her."

It's amazing to see how our heart changes when we look for ways to love our family. Something miraculous happens as we invest our hearts and our time in making our homes happy. Remember that it's cool to be close. Do the family thing—show your love now! Our families are the foundation of our futures, and even if you do not have the perfect mother or father, you can still learn from their mistakes. By doing so, someday you will be able to build your own family foundation through what you learned and through your faith in God.

If God wrote a love letter to you . . .

My beautiful girl—

I know how hard your family may be to love. But I am asking you to love them the way I love you . . . without condition. I will help you handle your family if you will come to Me in prayer so I can strengthen you. Your parents will sometimes upset you, and when this happens, I want you to forgive them quickly so a root of bitterness does not take root in your heart.

Love,
Your Daddy in heaven

Honor your father and mother, as the LORD your God has commanded you. Then you will live a long, full life in the land the LORD your God is giving you.

Deuteronomy 5:16

35

Protection

My dad would be the president of the Parents' Protection Club if there were such a thing. As a teenager, I thought he was a spy for the government or involved with underground crime, because he seemed so paranoid and protective of me. I was not allowed to leave my house without all the gear when I was a teen. He sent me out totally loaded with a bulletproof vest, rape alarm, Mace spray, beeper, cell phone, flashlight, stun gun, and a bunch of weird words of wisdom. Okay, I'm exaggerating a little bit, but you know how imprisoned you can feel by your parents' protection.

I used to resent my dad's overprotectiveness until one night when I was out with my girlfriends. Some guys were following us in their car and were actually threatening to kill us. We were flipped out and scared silly. Then I remembered my dad's weird words of wisdom. He said, "If strange guys ever follow you, don't drive home so that they will learn where you live. Call 911, then drive to the nearest police station." That's what we did, and those guys following us were arrested for harassment. My father's weird words of wisdom really worked!

My dad also often told me, "If it's dark, never walk out to your car alone. Ask someone to escort you." Then one night I saw a weird-looking man wandering around the mall parking lot. I was scared, and the mall was closing. My dad's weird words of wisdom haunted me once again. I found a security guard to walk me out. Later that night on the news, it was announced that two girls were murdered in that parking lot, right around the same time as I was leaving.

Even if your parent's words seem weird, listen! Their words could save you!

If God wrote a love letter to you . . .

My beautiful girl—

I have called you to be set apart. I know this calling will sometimes come with great cost, but the eternal rewards are worth much more than any pleasures of this world. I have given you parents to protect you, and I send My angels for your protection as well. Stay under the covering I have given you and you will save yourself much regret and pain. Some will admire you for your dedication to Me, and some will want you to fail rather than follow your lead. You may fall because you are not perfect, but your mistakes can be the tutors that make you wiser. All I ask is that you let Me set you apart so that I may use you as a witness for the world to see.

Love,
Your Daddy in heaven

He is a shield to those whose walk is
    blameless,
for he guards the course of the just
    and protects the way of his faithful ones.

Proverbs 2:7–8 NIV

36

Intercept Insults

Let's talk football. Even if you're not into the game, you can't help but hear the crowds cheer when someone intercepts a football in the middle of a play and begins running toward the opposite goal post.

I grew up around a lot of negative people. Many times we become what we surround ourselves with, so I began to become what people said about me. Kids can be cruel when you are not "Miss Popular." I did not know how to intercept their insults when I was young. I was a people-pleasing approval addict, so I could be wiped out with hurtful words easily. I had an English teacher who, in front of the class, told me that I was born to lose. My mother always pointed out how much better my friends were than me. My friends never encouraged me because they were just as messed up as I was. But something happened when I decided I was going to be a winner over their words. I didn't look to them for approval anymore. I looked to God for my confidence, and that made me strong enough to handle the hurtful tackles of their tongue.

We need to learn how to win the mind game over insensitive insults from others. You don't have to hand power over to people, friends, or family. Remember that hurting people hurt other people. Always consider the source before you allow anyone to destroy your confidence in who you are in Christ.

Today I've learned the intercept rules well. When someone insults me, I've learned to trust God to be my defense. In other words, stop talking, and eventually the insults will be intercepted by your silence. When someone says something bad about me to me, I look at the person and say, "I'm sorry you chose to believe that about me." Saying this intercepts the insult and returns the power to win back to you.

Pray for the person who insults you.

If God wrote a love letter to you . . .

My beautiful girl—

When anyone speaks hurtful words to you, they are coming against Me. You are My vessel of honor and a trophy of My grace. Look to Me for the truth when lies are spoken to you. Anyone who tries to hinder you will have to deal with Me, My love. Hide yourself in My treasured Word, and I will remind you of your immeasurable worth as many times as it takes. I am your faithful Father who fights for you. The battles you face are not yours; they are Mine to fight for you. I can take their insults and attacks, but you are too tender to handle this all alone. Just do the right thing and stand behind Me and you will find victory every time!

Love,
Your Daddy in heaven

Instead,

"If your enemies are hungry, feed them.
    If they are thirsty, give them something
    to drink.
In doing this, you will heap
    burning coals of shame on their heads."

Don't let evil conquer you, but conquer evil
by doing good.

Romans 12:20–21

37

What's the Deal with How We Feel?

Think about your favorite movie. Can you imagine watching that movie without any music soundtrack? We girls love music so much that it actually affects how we feel about the movie! We may even run right out to buy the movie soundtrack so we can relive that emotional movie experience again and again.

The soundtrack to our own individual movie of life has the same effect on us, good or bad. Emotions affect every fiber of our existence. There are times I feel so broken and emotionally hurt I don't see how God could ever use my pain for His purpose . . . but He does. Don't beat yourself up for how you feel; instead, learn to handle your heart and listen to the warnings that alert you to the presence of negative emotions (fear, anger, jealousy, depression, worry). Consider this plan of action for your reactions:

Let God have your heart. Pray immediately when negative emotions surface. Then on a piece of paper, write down what your feelings are and how those emotions made you feel and act. I've learned not to do anything until I've calmed down inside.

Seek out advice . . . from someone you trust who is older and wiser than you. Make sure that person loves you—and loves God and knows the Bible. Don't take advice from the wrong person; it could be a mistake you'll regret. Then once you have received good advice, write out your plan, and do it.

Do the right thing. I have learned that my best plan of action when I am out of control emotionally is to do the right thing whether I feel like it or not. When you feel like letting negative emotions take control of your mind and heart, choose to wait to react no matter how hard it seems at the time. This will always save you the pain of regret for reacting the wrong way.

If God wrote a love letter to you . . .

My beautiful girl—

What you may see as broken inside yourself, I see as beautiful. I am the One who makes beautiful things out of what is broken. I am the same God in your life who took a brokenhearted orphan named Esther and turned her into a queen who saved My people. Just as I used Esther's pain for My purpose, I will not waste a single tear you have shed, My love. I can and will use whatever is broken in your life for My glory. My love and mercy will shine brightest in those broken places. I will not only use what is broken, I will rebuild you to become even better and more beautiful than you could ever imagine.

Love,
Your Daddy in heaven

And we know that in all things God works for the good of those who love him, who have been called according to his purpose.

Romans 8:28 NIV

38

Facing Fear

There is good fear. Fear can be the very thing that saves us. *Fear of going to jail* can keep us from breaking the law. *Fear of getting pregnant or catching AIDS* can keep us sexually pure. *Fear of the future* can cause us to stay close to God. *Fear of failing* can be used as a motivator to make us do our best. *Fear of danger* can save our lives. *Fear of consequences for our actions* can keep us on the right road.

When I was in high school, I lived in constant fear of rejection. I could not handle the thought that some-one somewhere on my campus might not want to be my friend. This fear turned me into a people-pleasing approval addict. One time I was hanging out in front of a grocery store with some friends when they challenged me to go in to steal some candy. Some of them had already stolen some soda and cigarettes. Because I feared losing their friendship more than I feared being arrested for shoplifting candy, I went into the store. While I was waiting in line to buy some chips, I grabbed several candy bars and left quickly, expecting to receive the applause of my friends for my performance.

Instead I was met by two police officers—with handcuffs—who hauled me off to juvenile hall. As I rode in the back of that police car, all I could think about was how I had let fear force me to do something so stupid. I was not even the type of girl who liked to steal. Thankfully, my dad came to get me, and they dropped the "candy crime" charges.

Fear can cause us to react to things that will never happen. For example: Fear of losing a friend might make you act jealous and controlling toward that person. Fear of being fat has turned more than eight million girls bulimic. Fear of not being loved by a boy causes many girls to sleep with their boyfriends. The list of self-destruction caused by fear is endless.

Fear is the exact opposite of faith.

My beautiful daughter—

I know there is a hero hidden in your heart whether you believe it or not. I know this because I am the One who placed a desire in your soul to conquer fear and live with confidence in Me. The only thing that is holding you back from making a difference is you! Now, more than ever, your generation needs you to let go of fear and live every day with courage! I don't want My girl hiding behind fears and insecurities or paralyzed by what people think any more. You are My Princess Warrior, born to lead with your life, and I am your faithful Father, here to give you the courage to step out in faith and fight for what is right! Don't be afraid. I am with you always, fighting for you every day!

Love,
Your Daddy in heaven

So be strong and courageous! Do not be afraid and do not panic before them. For the LORD your God will personally go ahead of you. He will neither fail you nor abandon you.

Deuteronomy 31:6

39

A Beautiful Life

I had the honor of knowing a beautiful daughter of the King named Rachel. At the young age of thirteen, Rachel was diagnosed with cancer and given a very short time to live. I called Rachel as soon as I heard the news, and she said, "Sheri Rose, please pray that I can tell all my friends about Jesus before I die so I can see them all again." I was so touched by Rachel's beautiful heart. Although she was dying and her dreams on earth were ending, she cared more about giving her friends directions to where she was going.

On Rachel's sixteenth birthday, she announced, "I'm ready to go to heaven now. I finished my purpose here on earth." A few weeks later she died, but before she died, she wrote a very special letter to her friends. It read:

Dear friend, do not be sad for me today, because I am in Paradise where there is no more sickness and no more death, celebrating my eternal new life. My only wish is that I will get to see you someday and Jesus is your way to heaven.

Rachel's pastor invited kids to receive Christ that day, and hundreds from school prayed to receive the crown of life at her funeral. Rachel's beauty will be marked in her friends forever.

Ask yourself this question . . . If you were to die tomorrow, how would your friends and family remember you? What do you want people to remember you for?

I know I'm going deep right now, but your life was given to you for a divine purpose. God placed a gift inside of you. It's time to open it and give it away.

If God wrote a love letter to you . . .

My beautiful girl—

Your life lived for Me will become the legacy that lives on long after you are gone. Your fight will never be forgotten. You are a hero of the faith, and your commitment to the call will carve character in the next generation. Every prayer you prayed will become a blessing passed down. Every tough choice you made to obey Me will become a foundation of faith your family will stand on in their tough times. Your courage will continue to bring comfort to many during their difficult times. Your trust in Me will remain in others who watched you walk in peace. I, your God, declare on this day that your children's children will be forever blessed because you lived your life for an audience of One . . . Me!

Love,
Your Daddy in heaven

But I lavish unfailing love for a thousand generations on those who love me and obey my commands.

Exodus 20:6

40

The Ultimate Vacation

My dad started an advertising agency when I was a teenager, and his specialty was working with beautiful, five-star resort hotels in amazing places. Because these hotels were his accounts, he was given a big budget for free vacations. And I'm not just talking free rooms—I'm talking free food, free recreation, full use of the spa, tennis courts, swimming pool, and, of course, maid service and room service.

Every spring break I would invite my girlfriends on a paradise vacation totally paid for by my dad. These getaways were great vacations from my problems. I loved checking out of real life and into a hotel that had everything. I felt at home in these hotels and resorts.

One time while my friends and I were lying on the beach on a perfect sunny day, I said, "This is my life. Why can't I live it forever?" I had no idea at the time that there really is a place like Paradise where I can live forever, a place where I can have a permanent vacation from the pressures of life. In this Paradise we can hang out together in a place so peaceful that there, no one is stressed out, bummed out, or burned out. It is a place so safe there is no crime. It's so heartwarming and happy that it soothes your soul. There are angels and music so magical that it's like your favorite song times infinity. When you check into the Heavenly Hotel, you get an incredible free gift from God—you get to exchange your body for a perfect body that never gets sick and will never die. Love is always in the air, and no one can ever hurt you in any way.

Sounds too good to be true, doesn't it? Believe it or not, this heavenly place is a reality you can experience forever if you have the passport to get in. God has sent each of us a passport to paradise through His Son Jesus. But reading about God's love is not enough to secure a place in His eternal kingdom. We need to accept His invitation and receive the gift of His Son Jesus Christ.

I would love the privilege of being a part of your eternal crowning by asking you to say this simple prayer with me:

Dear God, I don't want to live without You any longer. I believe You sent Your Son to die for me and I want Him to be my Lord and my King. I confess my sin and my need for a Savior and I accept Your free gift of everlasting life. I thank You for writing my name in Your book of life.

I pray this prayer by faith in Jesus' name. Amen

If this is your sincere prayer, you can know that angels are rejoicing and the Holy Spirit of the Living God is now in you. Read the Scripture below and celebrate, because you are forever a part of the greatest family of all . . . God's family. You are a daughter of the King!

I tell you the truth, whoever hears my word and believes him who sent me has eternal life and will not be condemned; he has crossed over from death to life.

John 5:24 NIV

A Final Word from Sheri Rose

Now is your time to *shine* . . . to be the spotlight in someone's darkness. You will be the star that points to heaven. You will be the director who guides a lost soul back to God, and you'll be the audience for someone who needs to be applauded for their performance. Remember that the only thing that will matter when we are done with this life is that you made a difference. Don't lose your eternal perspective. Keep your eyes on heaven and your heart connected to God through prayer. When life hits hard, remember you are a Princess Warrior;

the fight for your faith is one that can and will be won in the power of the Holy Spirit inside of you.

We are not home yet. We are just visiting this place for the purpose of helping people find their eternal destination. You are not responsible for other's actions or reactions to God's great message, but you are responsible for your own actions. Remember that you can't change anyone but yourself. But your life can change the way people see the one God.

You are a treasure, and I pray you will see yourself for who you really are—a daughter of the Most High King.

I look forward to celebrating with you one day on the other side of eternity.

> May he give you the desire of your heart
> and make all your plans succeed.
> We will shout for joy when you are
> victorious
> and will lift up our banners in the name
> of our God.
>
> Psalm 20:4–5

Acknowledgments

I want to thank my loving, supportive husband, Steve, who takes care of me better than I could ever care for myself.

To my son, Jake, and my daughter-in-law, Amanda, thank you for praying for me.

To my best friends, Rochelle Pederson, Kimberly Engstrom, and Rhonda Funk—I am so blessed to have faithful friends like you in my life.

To my personal assistants, Whitney and Kelly—you are the best.

To my daughter, Emilie, the truest definition of a princess I know—thank you, girl, for praying for Mom everyday.

To my mother, Carole, and my stepmother, Susie—thanks for loving me.

To my daddy, Phil Goodman, thanks for always believing in me.

And last, thanks to my amazing editor, Lonnie, who has become family to me.

Sheri Rose Shepherd is the bestselling author of *His Princess, His Princess Bride, Fit for My King,* and several other books. She is a popular speaker and Bible teacher, and her teaching was the number one show of the year on *Focus on the Family*. Her life story about overcoming her struggles with weight and depression has been featured on the *Billy Graham Primetime Television Special*.

His Princess SERIES

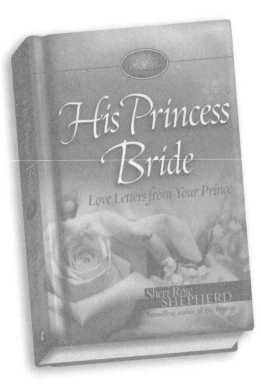

"Perfect for a gift. *His Princess Bride* will touch women's hearts at any age." —*Christian Retailing*

a division of Baker Publishing Group
www.RevellBooks.com

Stay connected with
Sheri Rose Shepherd
at www.hisprincess.com

- Friend her on Facebook.

- Follow her on Twitter.

- Read her blog.

- Sign up for her newsletter.

- Find a speaking event near you and see her live.